Signs of the Seasons

How Do You Know It's Spring?

by Ruth Owen

Consultants:

Suzy Gazlay, MA
Recipient, Presidential Award for Excellence in Science Teaching

Kimberly Brenneman, PhD
National Institute for Early Education Research, Rutgers University
New Brunswick, New Jersey

BEARPORT
PUBLISHING

NEW YORK, NEW YORK

Credits

Cover and Title Page, © Gabi Moisa/Shutterstock, and © Eric Gevaert/Shutterstock, and © Steve Byland/Shutterstock, and © Jessmine/Shutterstock; 4TL, © tomtsya/Shutterstock; 4BL, © Vaclav Volrab/Shutterstock; 4BR, © Jessmine/Shutterstock; 5BL, © Anat-oli/Shutterstock; 5, © Eric Gevaert/Shutterstock; 6, Mayovskyy Andrew/Shutterstock; 7, © Photononstop/Superstock; 8L, © Andrey Armyagov/Shutterstock; 8, © majeczka/Shutterstock; 9, © Anneka/Shutterstock; 9BR, © Evgeny Tomeev/Shutterstock; 10, © Filipe B. Varela/Shutterstock; 11TL, © Shutterstock; 11, © trgowanlock/Shutterstock; 12L, © Dani Vincek/Shutterstock; 12BL, © Andrei Rybachuk/Shutterstock; 12BR, © Anest/Shutterstock; 13, © Ulrich Mueller/Shutterstock; 14L, © Age Fotostock/Superstock; 14B, © Carsten Medom Madsen/Shutterstock; 15, © Design Pics/Superstock; 16TL, © Kevin E. Beasley/Shutterstock; 16BL, © ejwhite/Shutterstock; 16BC, © Steve Mann/Shutterstock; 16BR, © photosync/Shutterstock; 17, © Mike Truchon/Shutterstock; 18TL, © Wikipedia Creative Commons; 18BL, © Hans Lang/Imagebroker/FLPA; 18BR, © Gregory K. Scott/Science Photo Library; 19, © Peter Entwistle/FLPA; 20L, © Shutterstock; 20BC, © Losevsky Pavel/Shutterstock; 20R, © Shutterstock; 21, © Sergiy Bykhunenko/Shutterstock; 22TL, © Dani Vincek/Shutterstock; 22TC, © Peter Waters/Shutterstock; 22TR, © Cameramannz/Shutterstock; 22BL, © Devin Koob/Shutterstock; 22BR, © Subbotina Anna/Shutterstock; 23TL, © psamtik/Shutterstock; 23TC, © Anneka/Shutterstock; 23TR, © Peter Entwistle/FLPA; 23BL, © Design Pics/SuperStock; 23BC, © Ozerov Alexander/Shutterstock; 23BR, © Design Pics/SuperStock.

Publisher: Kenn Goin
Editorial Director: Adam Siegel
Creative Director: Spencer Brinker
Design: Emma Randall
Editor: Mark J. Sachner
Photo Researcher: Ruby Tuesday Books Ltd.

Library of Congress Cataloging-in-Publication Data

Owen, Ruth, 1967–
 How do you know it's spring? / by Ruth Owen.
  p. cm. — (Signs of the seasons)
 Includes bibliographical references and index.
 ISBN-13: 978-1-61772-398-8 (library binding)
 ISBN-10: 1-61772-398-3 (library binding)
 1. Spring—Juvenile literature. I. Title.
 QB637.5.O94 2012
 508.2—dc23
                      2011044373

For more information, write to Bearport Publishing Company, Inc., 45 West 21st Street, Suite 3B, New York, New York 10010. Printed in the United States of America in North Mankato, Minnesota.

10 9 8 7 6 5 4 3 2 1

Contents

It's Spring!

Every year there are four seasons—spring, summer, fall, and winter.

Spring begins just as winter comes to an end.

Many animals have their babies in spring.

It's the time of year when the weather warms up and plants begin to grow.

When you spot bright, yellow daffodils in a garden or park, it's a sign that spring is here!

crocuses

tulips

daffodils

Some of the first spring flowers are snowdrops, crocuses, daffodils, and tulips. Which spring flowers do you like best? Why?

4

Sheep give birth to their babies in late winter or early spring. One sign of spring is new lambs playing in sunny fields.

snowdrops

5

Goodbye, Winter Darkness

When winter begins, nighttime is much longer than daytime.

During winter, however, daytime begins to get a little longer each day.

By the time spring arrives, night and day are about the same length.

Then, all through spring, daytime is longer than nighttime.

Each year, spring starts on either March 20 or 21. The first day of spring is marked on calendars.

March

Su	M	T	W	Th	F	Sa
				1	2	3
4	5	6	7	8	9	10
11	12	13	14	15	16	17
18	19	20	21	22	23	24
25	26	27	28	29	30	31

first day of spring

Each week in spring, pick a day and draw a clock that shows what time it got dark. How much later does the sun set each week?

How early did it get dark?

Date	Sunset time
Mar 27	

Sunshine and Mud Puddles

Longer days are not the only clue that it's spring.

The weather also starts to feel warmer.

In some places there are rain showers, too.

rain showers

The warm spring weather can melt winter's snow and ice—and make lots of muddy puddles.

muddy puddles

Every Monday for four weeks during spring, use a thermometer to measure the temperature outside. Take your measurement at the same time of day. Make a chart to record your measurements. How does the temperature change from week to week?

Weather Chart

Date	Temperature
April 1	60°F (16°C)
April 8	62°F (17°C)
April 15	65°F (18°C)
April 22	67°F (19°C)

9

Little Green Signs

In winter, it is too cold for many plants to grow.

The plants' leaves and flowers die, but their **roots** are still alive underground.

In spring, the warmer weather makes the plants grow again.

One sign of spring is new green plant **shoots** pushing up through the soil.

Seeds begin to grow into new plants when the spring weather warms up the soil.

seed

plant shoot

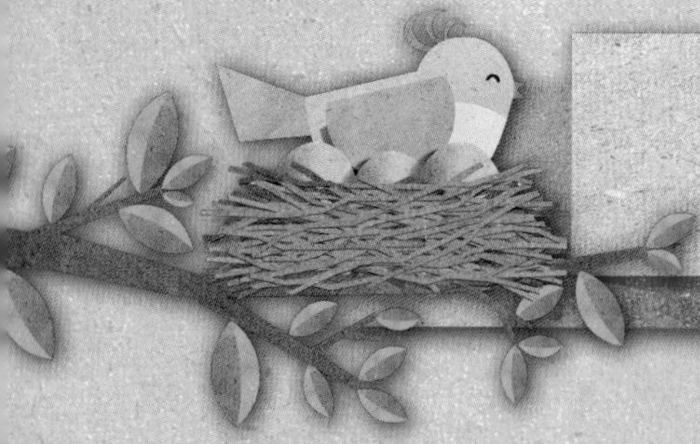

Buds and Blossoms

In winter, many trees have lost all their leaves.

In spring, fat green **buds** begin growing on the bare branches.

When the buds burst open, new leaves and flowers uncurl from inside!

branch

buds

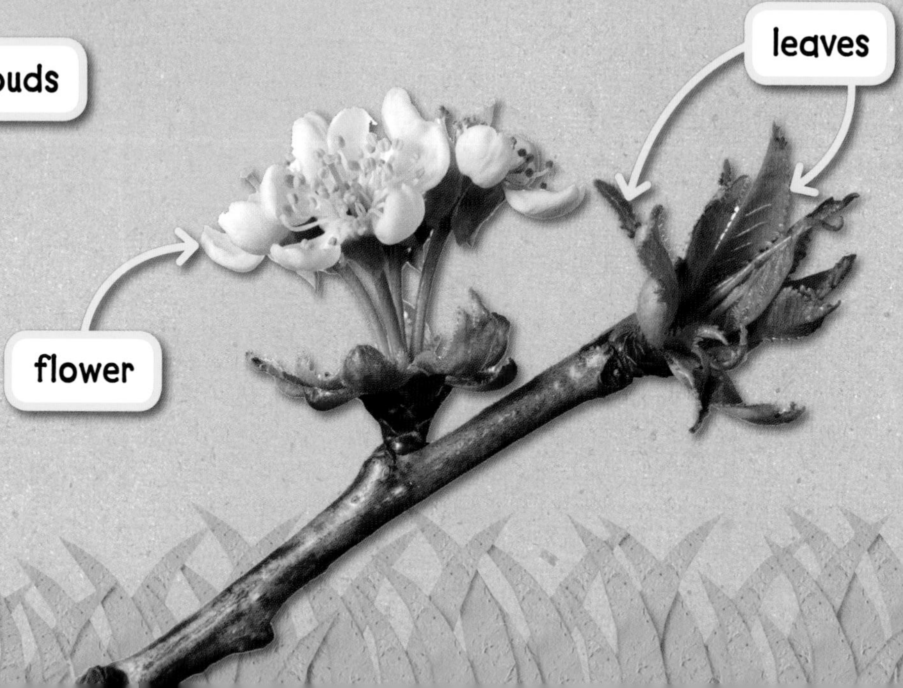

leaves

flower

In spring, fruit trees grow beautiful flowers called blossoms.

blossoms

Ask a grown-up to cut a small branch with buds from a tree or bush. Place the branch in water. Draw what you see when the buds burst open.

Hungry Babies

On a sunny spring day, a mother squirrel and her babies look for food in a park.

They find buds, new leaves, flowers, and juicy **insects** to eat.

There is plenty of food around.

That's why many animals have their babies in spring.

bud

baby squirrel

mother squirrel

baby raccoons

Squirrels, raccoons, chipmunks, rabbits, and many other animals give birth in spring.

During spring, look for animal families playing and collecting food in parks and backyards. In a notebook, draw and label the animals you see.

Busy Birds

Birds collect grass and twigs in spring to build nests for their eggs.

A female robin sits on her eggs to keep them warm.

When the chicks **hatch**, the mother and father feed them insects and worms.

a robin collecting grass

robin egg

nest

Leave yarn or shredded paper outside. Watch to see which birds take it for building nests.

Egg Hunting

In spring, you might see butterfly eggs on leaves.

Wriggly caterpillars hatch from the eggs.

In a few weeks, the caterpillars will change into butterflies.

butterfly eggs

caterpillar

frog eggs

In spring, frogs lay their eggs in ponds. Each tiny black egg is inside a blob of jelly.

butterfly

19

Spring in a Garden

When spring arrives, many people plant seeds to grow flowers and vegetables.

In a few weeks, the seeds start to grow into plants.

In summer, there will be colorful flowers to see, and vegetables to pick and dig up.

Spring is the season for planting so that there will be good things to eat later in the year!

Garden Seeds
Cosmos
A Butterfly Favorite!

Garden Seeds
Sunflower
Sunny Giants

Garden Seeds
Tomatoes
Sweet and Juicy

Garden Seeds
Carrots
Crunchy and Sweet

buying seeds at a garden center

Spring is a great time to be outside. What signs of spring can you spot? What sounds do you hear? What can you smell?

Spring lasts until June 20 or 21. That is when summer begins!

21

Science Lab

When you are playing in your backyard, on the playground at school, or in the park, go on a spring treasure hunt.

See how many of the things on the Spring Treasure Hunt list you can see, smell, hear, or collect.

If it's not spring where you live, then draw a picture of a spring scene.

Include as many things from the list as you can.

Then when spring comes to where you live, go outside and try to find the things you included in your drawing.

Spring Treasure Hunt

Things to see
Green shoots
A bud on a tree branch
A tree with blossoms
A caterpillar
A butterfly
A bird collecting food
Frog eggs in a pond

Things to collect
Something a bird could use to build a nest
A small bunch of spring flowers
A twig with a bud

Things to smell
A flower
Tree blossoms
The air after a rain shower

Things to hear
Rain pattering on an umbrella
Baby birds chirping in a nest

Science Words

buds (BUDZ) small growths on the stems of trees and other plants that flowers and leaves grow from

hatch (HACH) to break out of an egg

insects (IN-sekts) small animals that have six legs, two antennas, an exoskeleton, and three main body parts

roots (ROOTS) long, thin, underground parts of plants that take in food and water from the soil

seeds (SEEDZ) tiny parts of a plant that can grow into a new plant

shoots (SHOOTS) new growing parts of a plant that appear from underground

23

Index

Read More

Esbaum, Jill. *Everything Spring.* Washington, D.C.: National Geographic (2010).

Glaser, Linda. *It's Spring! (Celebrate the Seasons).* Minneapolis, MN: Millbrook Press (2002).

Latta, Sara L. *What Happens in Spring? (I Like the Seasons!).* Berkeley Heights, NJ: Enslow (2006).

Learn More Online

To learn more about spring, visit **www.bearportpublishing.com/SignsoftheSeasons**

About the Author

Ruth Owen has been writing children's books for more than ten years. She particularly enjoys working on books about animals and the natural world. Ruth lives in Cornwall, England, just minutes from the ocean. She loves gardening and caring for her family of llamas.